SUPER
SANDCASTLE®
State Stories

THE APPLE STATE TREASURE HUNT

~ A Story About Washington ~

Written by Katherine Hengel

Illustrated by Bob Doucet

Consulting Editor, Diane Craig, M.A./Reading Specialist

A Division of ABDO
ABDO
Publishing Company

visit us at www.abdopublishing.com

Published by ABDO Publishing Company, a division of ABDO, P.O. Box 398166, Minneapolis, Minnesota 55439. Copyright © 2011 by Abdo Consulting Group, Inc. International copyrights reserved in all countries. No part of this book may be reproduced in any form without written permission from the publisher. Super SandCastle™ is a trademark and logo of ABDO Publishing Company.

Printed in the United States of America, North Mankato, Minnesota
112010
012011

 PRINTED ON RECYCLED PAPER

Editor: Liz Salzmann
Content Developer: Nancy Tuminelly
Cover and Interior Design: Anders Hanson, Mighty Media
Production: Colleen Dolphin, Oona Gaarder-Juntti, Mighty Media
Photo Credits: Bob Doucet, One Mile Up, Quarter-dollar coin image from the United States Mint, Shutterstock

Library of Congress Cataloging-in-Publication Data

Hengel, Katherine.
  The Apple State treasure hunt : a story about Washington /
Katherine Hengel ; illustrated by Bob Doucet.
    p. cm. -- (Fact & fable: state stories)
  ISBN 978-1-61714-679-4
  1. Washington (State)--Juvenile literature. I. Doucet, Bob, ill. II.
Title.
  F891.3.H46 2011
  979.7--dc22
                              2010022173

Super SandCastle™ books are created by a team of professional educators, reading specialists, and content developers around five essential components—phonemic awareness, phonics, vocabulary, text comprehension, and fluency—to assist young readers as they develop reading skills and strategies and increase their general knowledge. All books are written, reviewed, and leveled for guided reading, early reading intervention, and Accelerated Reader® programs for use in shared, guided, and independent reading and writing activities to support a balanced approach to literacy instruction.

TABLE OF CONTENTS

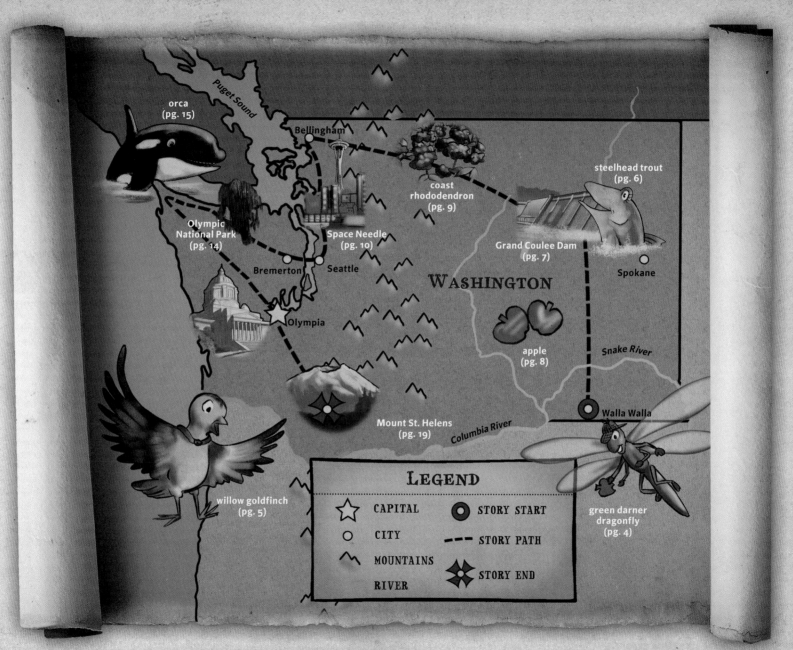

orca
(pg. 15)

Puget Sound

Bellingham

coast
rhododendron
(pg. 9)

steelhead trout
(pg. 6)

Olympic
National Park
(pg. 14)

Space Needle
(pg. 10)

Grand Coulee Dam
(pg. 7)

Bremerton   Seattle

Spokane

WASHINGTON

Olympia

apple
(pg. 8)

Snake River

Mount St. Helens
(pg. 19)

Columbia River

Walla Walla

willow goldfinch
(pg. 5)

green darner
dragonfly
(pg. 4)

LEGEND

☆ CAPITAL   ◉ STORY START

○ CITY   - - - STORY PATH

⋀ MOUNTAINS   ✦ STORY END

RIVER

3

Green Darner Dragonfly

The green darner looks kind of like a **darning** needle! That's how it got its name. The green darner is one of the largest dragonflies in the world. It is the state **insect** of Washington.

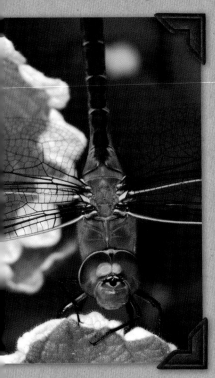

4

THE APPLE STATE TREASURE HUNT

Drew Dragonfly holds his breath as Miss Purdy announces the teams. His heart stops when he hears his name. "Drew, you are with Garrett," Miss Purdy says.

Garrett Goldfinch is the new kid in the Walla Walla Treasure Trackers club. Drew lets out a large sigh. "I wish we didn't have to work in teams this year," he thinks to himself.

"Ok, find your **partners** and get your maps! Remember, each team gets a different treasure map!" Miss Purdy says.

Garrett approaches Drew. "Hello, I'm Garrett!" he **chirps**. "I'm so very glad we're partners. I hear that you are the best treasure tracker in all of Washington!"

"Let's hope so," Drew says. "Come on. Let's grab our map and get started."

Walla Walla
Treasure Trackers Club

Willow Goldfinch

The willow goldfinch is also called the American goldfinch. It is the state bird of Washington. It is very social! Willow goldfinches like to feed and **migrate** together. They even like people! They are often found in neighborhoods that have many birdfeeders!

Steelhead Trout

The steelhead trout is often called rainbow trout. A steelhead trout doesn't forget where it was born. It returns to its birthplace when it is ready to lay eggs! The steelhead trout is the state fish of Washington.

They travel north toward the first treasure. As they fly over the Snake River, Garrett sees a fish.

"Are you a steelhead trout?" he asks.

"Yes! Tina Trout is my name."

"I'm Garrett Goldfinch and this is Drew Dragonfly!"

Garrett stops to visit with Tina Trout. He even shares some of his mother's famous Washington trail mix with her!

"How will I ever cross the state with this chatty bird?" Drew thinks.

Washington Trail Mix

1 cup diced dried fruit, such as apples, pears, and apricots

½ cup raisins

1½ cups unsalted sunflower seeds

½ cup chocolate chips

1 cup peanuts

Combine all of the ingredients in a bowl. Mix well. Divide the mixture into small plastic bags. Enjoy this trial mix at home or on the go!

They continue north to the Columbia River. They follow it to the Grand Coulee Dam. Drew is nervous. "We lost some time at the river," he says. "Let's work quickly."

Drew finds the first treasure near the riverbank. It's a small plastic apple with "Walla Walla Treasure Trackers" written on it. Inside is their first sticker.

"Wow, that's great!" **chirps** Garrett. "We have to find four more stickers, right?"

Drew nods as he places the sticker on the map. "No one else is going to the same places we are!"

Grand Coulee Dam

The Grand Coulee Dam is on the Columbia River. It is the largest concrete **structure** in the United States! It is almost 1 mile (1.6 km) long. The force of the flowing water is used to make electricity.

7

Apple

The apple is the state fruit of Washington. Washington produces more than 60 percent of the apples sold in the United States. Apple trees originally came from central Asia. There are more than 7,500 types of apples.

Their next treasure is in Bellingham. "That's all the way across the state," Drew explains.

"What is the prize?" Garrett asks.

"It's a year's supply of Washington apples. The first person, I mean, the first team to get all five stickers wins."

"Wow!" Garrett exclaims. "Can that many apples really grow in Washington?"

"Of course!" Drew says. "Most of the apples in United States come from Washington!"

The two fly for a long time over farms and then mountains. They arrive in Bellingham, and Drew quickly finds the second treasure. It's in a beautiful bed of coast rhododendron near a highway.

"This is Highway 5," Drew says. "We can follow it all the way to our next treasure in Seattle!"

Coast Rhododendron

The Washington state flower is the coast rhododendron. This flowering bush can be 7 to 30 feet (2 to 9 m) tall! The flowers are usually pink. They are common on roadsides along the Pacific Coast.

Space Needle

The Space Needle is a famous tower in Seattle. It is 605 feet (184 m) high. Visitors can take an elevator to the top! It was built for the World's Fair in 1962.

Garrett likes Seattle. "What a great city!" he exclaims. "Look at that building!"

"That's the Space Needle," says Drew. "Our next treasure is near it."

"I hope it takes awhile for us to find our treasure here!"

Drew shakes his head. "You're a funny one."

"Check it out!" Garrett yells. "There's a band playing in that park!" Before Drew can say no, Garrett is off to Seattle Center.

Drew flies to catch up with him. As he arrives at the park, he notices the third treasure under a bench.

"I found it!" Drew exclaims. Garrett didn't hear him. He was too close to the band! Drew flies over to Garrett. He says, "We better head to the docks. We have a **ferry** to catch."

"All right," Garrett says. "But we have to come back here some time!"

Seattle Center

The Seattle Center is a fairground, park, and entertainment center. It is 74 **acres** (30 ha). The International Fountain is in the middle. The fountain shoots water in time with world music!

11

Puget Sound

Puget Sound is a large **inlet** in northeastern Washington. It is made up of many waterways connected to the Pacific Ocean. Orcas, salmon, seals, and sea lions live in the sound.

The two treasure trackers fly to the Seattle Terminal on Puget Sound. "I'm glad we're taking a **ferry**," Garrett says as they board. "I'm tired of flying!"

"Me too," Drew **admits**. "It's good to stay rested on these treasure hunts. That's a big part of my plan actually. It's one of my secrets."

Just then, Drew realizes something that makes his heart sink. "Oh, no! I don't have the map," he says quietly.

Garrett is stunned, but tries to be helpful. "Let's see. We had it in the park. You must have lost it on the way to the **ferry**."

Drew stares out at a large ship in the water. "We'll be okay," Drew says. "The map said Olympic something."

Washington State Ferries

The state of Washington has a special ferry system. It has more ferries than any other in the United States! The ferries help people who live near Puget Sound get around!

13

Olympic National Park

In the middle of Olympic National Park are the Olympic Mountains. There are sandy beaches and rocky cliffs on the coast. The west side of the park has rainforests. The Hall of Mosses is a trail through the rainforest.

They get off the **ferry** and fly to Olympic National Park. They land in the Hall of Mosses.

"This forest is so huge," Garrett says. "We'll never find the treasure here."

They head north until they reach the Pacific Ocean.

"We're lost," says Drew. "I'm sorry I lost the map."

"Don't worry," Garrett says. "We'll think of something."

Suddenly, a huge orca rises up out of the ocean. "Did I hear that you are looking for a map?" says Orion Orca.

"Yes!" Garrett says. "We're Walla Walla treasure trackers, and we lost our map."

"I saw a map over there on the beach," Orion says. "Maybe it's yours."

Drew flies to the map. "This is it! The wind must have blown it here. But we were supposed to go to Olympia, not Olympic National Park!" he exclaims.

Orca

The orca is the state **marine mammal** of Washington. Orcas are sometimes called killer whales. They are found in all the oceans of the world.

15

Olympia

Olympia is the capital of Washington. It is a large city near Puget Sound. It has many theaters for plays and music and dance **performances**. The main **capitol** building is the Legislative Building. It was completed in 1928.

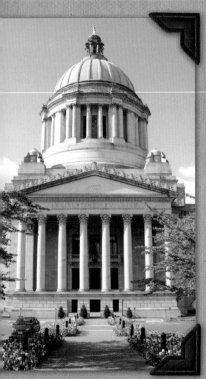

"It's like when folks mistake Washington, D.C., for Washington state!" says Orion Orca. "Good luck!"

Drew and Garrett fly as fast as they can to Olympia. "Looks like our next treasure is near the capitol," Drew says.

The two treasure trackers search around the outside of the capitol. Garrett sees the little red apple near a bush! "I found it!" he exclaims.

"Nice work!" Drew says. "I'm **impressed**! Now we're off to find our last treasure in the mountains!"

Garrett smiles. He's proud that he was able to help. "That mountain?" he asks.

"No, that's Mount Rainier," Drew says. "We're going to a different mountain. Follow me!"

The two friends fly southeast. Drew holds the map tightly as they fly. "I sure don't want to lose it again!" he says.

Mount Rainier

Mount Rainier is a large, active **volcano**. It is also called Mount Tahoma. It is located 54 miles (87 km) southeast of Seattle. It is the highest mountain in Washington.

Cascade Range

The Cascade Range is a major mountain range in North America. It runs from British Columbia to northern California. It includes several active **volcanoes**! Mount Rainier and Mount St. Helens are both in the Cascade Range.

They land near the base of a beautiful mountain. "Here we are," Drew says. "This is Mount St. Helens."

"We've flown over so many mountains," Garrett says. "Are they all connected?"

"Yes" Drew says. "They're all part of the Cascade Range. Flying over them is one thing. Now we have to search them! Treasure tracking on a mountain can be very hard."

"Do you think we'll find the last treasure?" Garrett asks.

Drew hands the map to Garrett.

"Only if you hold on to the map!"

Garrett is surprised and pleased. "Are you sure, Drew?" he asks.

"I'm sure. You're ready for Mount St. Helens," Drew says. "You've really proven yourself. I'll be your **partner** any day!"

THE END

Mount St. Helens

Mount St. Helens is an active **volcano**. It is 96 miles (154 km) south of Seattle. Mount St. Helens is famous for **erupting** on May 18, 1980. It was the deadliest volcano eruption in United States history.

WASHINGTON AT A GLANCE

Abbreviation: WA

Capital: Olympia

Largest city: Seattle

Statehood: November 11, 1889
(42nd state)

Area: 68,097 square miles
(176,370 sq km)
(21st-largest state)

Nickname: Evergreen State

Motto: Al-ki — By and By

State flower:
coast rhododendron

State tree: western hemlock

State bird: willow goldfinch

State insect: green darner
dragonfly

State fish: steelhead trout

State marine mammal: orca

State fruit: apple

State song:
"Washington, My Home"

STATE SEAL

STATE QUARTER

The Washington State Quarter
shows a king salmon jumping
out of the water. Mount Rainier
is in the background.

STATE FLAG

WHAT DO YOU KNOW?

How well do you remember the story? Match the pictures to the
questions below! Then check your answers at the bottom of the page!

a. Mount
St. Helens

b. apples

c. Garrett
Goldfinch

d. Grand Coulee
Dam

e. Orion Orca

f. green darner
dragonfly

1. What kind of animal is Drew?

2. Where do Drew and Garrett find their
first treasure?

3. What is the prize for winning the
treasure hunt?

4. Who helps Drew and Garrett find their
map?

5. Who finds the treasure in Olympia?

6. Where is the final treasure?

What to Do in Washington

1 **Visit a World Expo Pavilion**

Riverfront Park,
Spokane

5 **Shop at a Famous Waterfront Market**

Pikes Place Market,
Seattle

2 **Pick Fruit at an Apple Orchard**

Prey's Fruit Barn,
Leavenworth

6 **Go Whale Watching**

San Juan Islands

3 **See a Rocky Mountain Elk**

Oak Creek
Cowiche

7 **Watch Snow Geese Migrate**

Bellingham

4 **Hike a Mountain Trail**

Mount Rainier National Park

8 **Discover a Mountain Lake**

Hidden Lake Trail,
North Cascades National Park

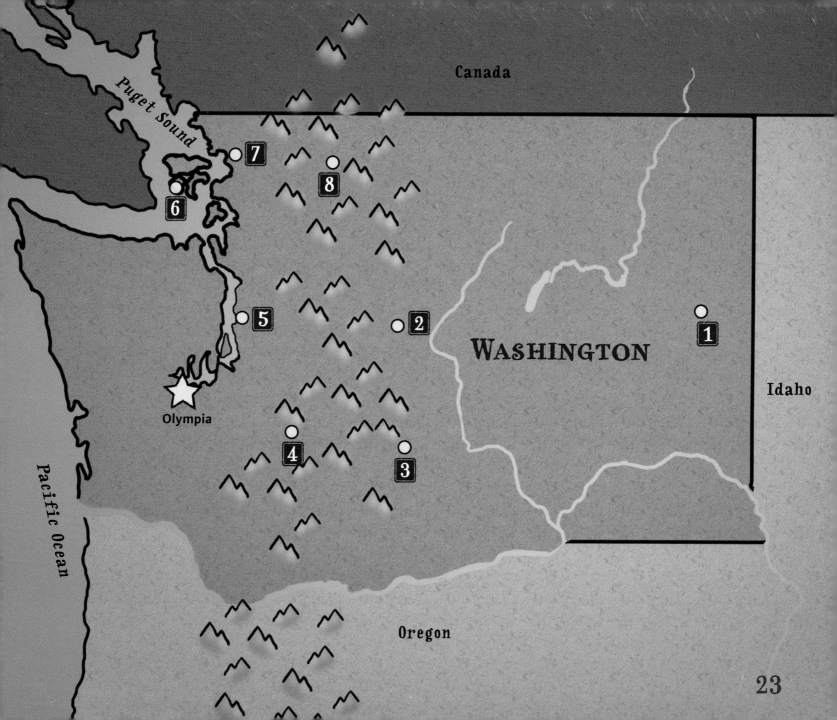

Canada

Puget Sound

7

8

6

5

2

WASHINGTON

1

Idaho

Pacific Ocean

Olympia

4

3

Oregon

GLOSSARY

acre – a unit of measurement that equals 43,560 square feet (4,047 sq m). One acre is a little smaller than a football field.

admit – to say that something is so.

capitol – a building where state laws are made.

chirp – the sound a bird or insect makes.

darning – a method of sewing used to fix holes.

erupt – to explode. A volcano *eruption* is when lava and ashes shoot out of a volcano.

ferry – a boat that takes people and cars across a body of water.

impress – to get someone's attention or interest.

inlet – a narrow strip of water between islands or running inland from a larger body of water.

insect – a small creature with two or four wings, six legs, and a body with three sections.

mammal – a warm-blooded animal that has hair and whose females produce milk to feed their young.

marine – having to do with the sea.

migrate – to move from one area to another, usually at about the same time each year.

partner – someone you work on a project or job with.

performance – the act of doing something in front of an audience.

structure – something that has been built, such as a house, a bridge, a hospital, or a tower.

volcano – a mountain that has lava and ash inside of it.